Tablet Weaving

Tablet Weaving

Ann Sutton
and Pat Holtom

B T Batsford Limited   London and Sydney

Photographs by Sam Sawdon
Sketches on pages 46 and 47 by Dot Henderson

©Ann Sutton and Pat Holtom 1975
First Published 1975

ISBN 0 7134 2891 0

Filmset by Tradespools Limited
Frome, Somerset
Printed and bound in Great Britain
by William Clowes and Sons Limited
Beccles, Suffolk
for the publishers B T Batsford Limited
4 Fitzhardinge Street, London W1H 0AH
23 Cross Street Brookvale
NSW 2100 Australia

Contents

To Vicky and the Xaghra weavers

Silk pincushion with inscription 'God
bless P C (for Prince Charles) and down
with the Rump'. Mid 17th century. From
the London Museum

Introduction

Tablet weaving or card weaving is an ancient method of producing strong elaborately patterned woven braids without using a loom. At one time these braids were used for decorative saddlery, bridles and reins, garters, sword-belts, or for tying up scrolls, but now the same techniques can be used to produce bands for dress and furnishing uses, hatbands, ties, belts and many other items. Joined side-by-side, the braids have many more uses. The technique of lettering in tablet weaving, traditionally used to convey loyal and loving messages, can now be used to inscribe, for example, guitar straps.

The equipment is simple (originally a few old playing cards, now plastic tablets) and the patterns produced are amongst the most complicated in textile production. It is one of the very few textile techniques which have never been mechanised, and the production of these braids can be a fascinating introduction to hand-weaving for non-weavers, or for weavers an exploration into a technique which has many exciting possibilities.

Ordinary weaving with 6 warp threads

Tablet weaving with 12 warp threads, ie 3 tablets of 4 threads each

Origin

If four threads are threaded through four holes in a piece of card, and stretched between two supports:

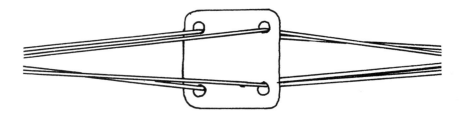

and the card is twisted:

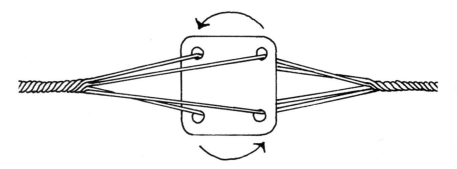

a strong cord will result from the twisting together of these four 'warp' threads.

Because tablet weaving originated so long ago, it is only possible to guess that when a strong flat band was needed as an animal girth, several cords were attached to each other side-by-side; probably a thread would have been threaded through each cord with a needle. A logical next step would have been the realisation that by *making* the cords side-by-side, a weft thread could be passed through with every twist of the tablets, joining the cords together automatically and forming the strong braid needed.

Notes on the history of tablet weaving

The earliest piece of tablet weaving in existence is Egyptian: bands of linen and ramie dating from the 22nd Dynasty (945–745 BC). However, it has been suggested by Professor A Van Gennep that a study of the geometric bands depicted on Ancient Egyptian clothing in contemporary painting and sculpture show that tablet weaving was skilfully practised in 3000 BC.

The Girdle of Rameses (1200 BC), now in Liverpool Museum, is probably the most mysterious piece of weaving in the world. For many years experts have argued about the method of its production, and many have woven copies to 'prove' that it was tablet woven. It is a very large piece, and some historians think that it was woven not for Rameses to wear but for his elephant. It is 5·2 m (17 ft) long, and at one end it is 127 mm (5 in.) wide, tapering evenly down to the other end which is 48 mm ($1\frac{7}{8}$ in.) wide. There are about 300 linen warp threads per inch. If indeed it was woven by tablet weaving, it is curious that no pre-Copt tablets have ever been found, and it seems unlikely that the technique should have reached these heights in intricacy, only to fall back and re-emerge later in the simpler forms dated around 950 BC. One thing, however, resulted from the attempts to weave replicas with tablets: a large number of ingenious patterns were evolved in the process.

Egyptian band. From the Victoria and Albert Museum

right Girdle of Rameses. From the City of Liverpool Museums

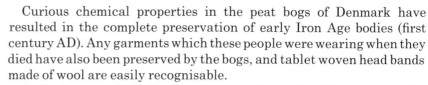

Curious chemical properties in the peat bogs of Denmark have resulted in the complete preservation of early Iron Age bodies (first century AD). Any garments which these people were wearing when they died have also been preserved by the bogs, and tablet woven head bands made of wool are easily recognisable.

At Oseburg, on Oslo fjord in Norway, the tomb of Queen Asa (who died about AD 850) was opened, and a set of 52 wooden tablets threaded and with the braid half-woven was discovered.

Between AD 600 and 1100, German tablet weaving reached very high standards: fine threads were used, abundant amounts of gold thread, and many inscriptions were woven into the braids. Saint Cuthbert died in AD 687, and his vestments in Durham Cathedral are trimmed with braids tablet woven in Germany.

One of the finest pieces of tablet weaving in existence is the Girdle of Saint Witgarius, now in Augsberg. Its beautifully woven inscription tells that it was a gift from Hemma, consort of Lewis the German, to Bishop Witgar in the latter part of the ninth century.

Bronze Age belt from Borum Eshoj, Denmark. Woven on 2 hole tablets; 4 hole tablets first came into use in the early Iron Age. From the National Museum, Copenhagen, Denmark

right Set of tablets, threaded and with half completed braid, from the tomb of Queen Asa. From the Collection of Antiquities, Oslo University, Norway

Bishop Witgar's girdle. From the Diocesan
Museum, Augsberg, Germany

above Inscription band, tablet woven in red silk in Upper Germany. Early medieval. From the Diocesan Museum, Augsberg, Germany

right Caucasian band. From the Museum für Völkerkunde, Saint Gallen

below Turkish bands in worsted showing the weaver's trial turnings on the left. The other end shows the preferred pattern, which continues for the whole length

A medieval German law stated that anyone injuring the hand of a tablet weaver must pay a fine of five-quarters the amount due to any other persons injured.

Gold belts and braids were tablet woven by men in the workshops of armourers in Russian Georgia, 1897, and Caucasian tablets made from playing cards were shown in a Russian museum at that time.

Margarethe Lehmann-Filhés documented the history of tablet weaving in 1899 in Berlin. She had become passionately interested in Icelandic weaving, which was technically advanced and used the 'two turns away, two towards' technique, as described later in *Lettering*. Miss Lehmann-Filhés' research into the technique of tablet weaving in general and her subsequent briefing of explorers brought in news of the craft from all parts of the world. In 1902 an exhibition and demonstrations of tablet weaving were held in the Berlin Arts and Crafts Museum, and a 'craze' resulted, with patterns appearing in Ladies' Magazines at the time.

Tablet weaving has remained popular in many parts of the world. In Palestine tablet-woven bands with inscriptions such as 'Jerusalem' were being sold to tourists in this century. In Greece the red garters

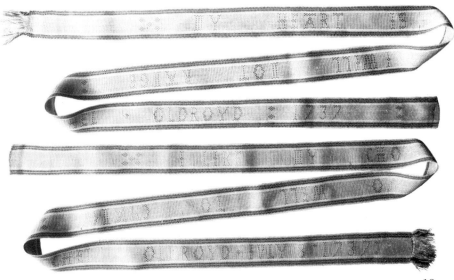

Tablet woven silk garters (a love token) with the inscriptions 'My heart is fixt I will not range Rachel Oldroyd 1737' and 'I like my choyce to well to change Rachel Oldroyd July 8 1737'. From the London Museum

in the national costume are tablet woven. In North Africa tablet woven bands are still made for trimming djellabahs and for harness straps. These bands for trimming clothing are made of rayon. Several tablet weavers work in the souks in Meknes, Morocco. One man will weave two 5·5 m (6 yd) warps per day, using a simple weaving-stand placed on the ground.

Although tablet weaving has never been properly mechanised, Arthur Lee of Birkenhead, produced prototype machines for braid production during the First World War. He used cogged discs instead of tablets (gleaned from gas metres because of the shortage of metal at the time). Pedals turned ridged rollers, which located into the notched edges of the disc tablets and revolved them into the next position. At least one of these machines is still in existence.

North African loom. From the Museum für Völkerkunde, Hamburg

Part one

This part of the book is planned for beginners who do not wish to become involved in buying equipment and are content to weave shorter lengths and small articles. For the work described in Part Two, a loom and some experience of weaving or tablet weaving would be useful.

For most pieces of tablet weaving it is essential to follow a specific draft (pattern), and to thread up and weave accurately. It is wise to avoid distractions at all stages, but especially at the beginning, and a complete understanding of the chapter *How to start* (page 19) is necessary before satisfactory work can be done. A few beginners find difficulty in turning the tablets through the threads: the secret is to hold them in a relaxed way, gently but firmly, and not to grip them tightly. Persevere, without a weft thread, until a positive action is found.

The words used throughout the book to denote direction are 'towards' and 'away', as in the methods described in this book the weaver is sitting in a position looking down the length of the warp, whether weaving from a chair to a fixed point, or on a loom. In other books the terms used might be 'right, left', 'backwards, forwards', 'clockwise, anticlockwise', etc.

Materials

The warp threads are more important than the weft threads in tablet weaving. They provide the colour and texture, and the weft thread shows only at the edges of the braid. These warp threads have to be smooth, so that projecting fibres do not catch together and bind up the threads during the twisting, and strong, to take the strain and tension of weaving. They should not be too wiry or too soft. The weft thread need not be the same as the warp but should match the edge threads in colour wherever possible. The thickness of the weft thread can affect the proportion of the pattern.

The beginner will find that a mercerised knitting cotton such as *Lyscord, Lyscordet* or *Stalite* (available from most knitting wool shops) will be good, trouble-free material with which to learn the technique. For small items, embroidery cottons such as *Clark's Anchor Pearl, Anchor Soft,* or stranded cottons work well and come in extensive colour ranges.

In wool, crêpe yarns give a good result but tend to stretch during weaving. Wools which are spun by the worsted method with very few projecting fibres are ideal. Knobbly wools should be avoided at this stage.

More suggestions for materials are given in Part Two, but these are not recommended for beginners. Suppliers of suitable materials in larger quantities are listed at the back of the book.

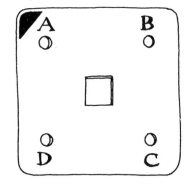

Equipment

The equipment for tablet weaving is very simple: a pack of square cards or tablets, now usually made of thin plastic, commercially. Each measures between 50 mm (2 in.) and 75 mm (3 in.) square, and up to 1·5 mm ($\frac{1}{16}$ in.) thick, with rounded corners and smooth surfaces everywhere, so that nothing can catch up in the threads causing snags and mistakes. There is a 1·5 mm ($\frac{1}{16}$ in.) hole in each corner, lettered A,B,C,D, in a clockwise direction. Some identifying symbol is desirable in the A corner.

These tablets are also easy to make, out of thin, good quality card. Old playing cards are ideal for the purpose, and have been used for tablet weaving all over the world for centuries. Cut them to form squares, rounding off the two cut corners, and punch holes near but not too close to the corners with an office punch. It is important that a punch is used for these holes, because the edge of the hole, as well as the card surfaces and edges, must be as smooth as possible.

It is convenient, but not essential, to have a hole about 13 mm ($\frac{1}{2}$ in.) square in the centre of each tablet, and to keep a piece of string or tape nearby when weaving; this can be threaded through the central holes and tied when work is stopped temporarily, and stops the tablets getting out of order if the warp is slackened.

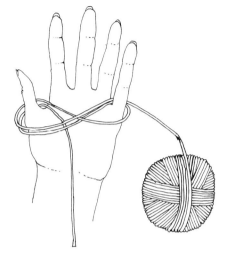

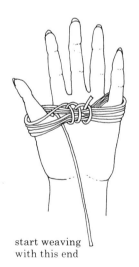

start weaving
with this end

Up to 50 tablets (depending on the thickness of the threads) can be used together without needing a loom to keep the threads taut, but with the use of a loom up to 100 tablets can be handled with ease, depending on the thickness of the thread used and on the size of the tablets. British tablets tend to be smaller than American tablets, and can be handled in larger numbers.

Obviously fine threads will need more tablets to produce a wide braid. Thick threads will use fewer tablets for the same width braid.

For work similar to that shown in the first part of this book, however, a set of about 20 cards, an immovable tying point such as a doorknob or tree to support the warp, and the weaver's chair will be sufficient equipment. In Part Two there is a chapter describing other equipment which is desirable if wider braids or some of the variations are attempted.

The weft thread must be packaged so that it does not tangle. It can be wound on to a small piece of card or made into a 'dolly'. See diagrams left.

If a dolly is used, a ruler will be useful for beating the weft threads into position, ie pressing the weft thread firmly up against the previous weft thread.

The ideal set of equipment includes a Norwegian belt shuttle, as it combines a weft carrier with a blade for beating. Because the shuttle is thicker at the top than at the blade, bulky build-up of yarn does not obstruct the beating up of the weft, as it would if a netting shuttle or stick shuttle were used.

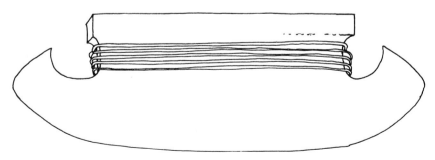

A Norwegian belt shuttle

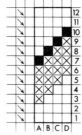

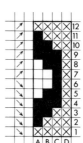

Diamond
This design needs
16 dark threads
12 medium threads
20 light threads

Wave
This design needs
4 dark threads
16 medium threads
28 light threads

Flower
This design needs
18 dark threads
2 medium threads
6 light threads

18

How to start

Choose one of the designs on the opposite page. Underneath each one is a list of the number of threads needed for each colour. Cut threads 1·2 m (4 ft) long for the pattern chosen, and try to keep them in a neat bundle with the ends even.

Reading the pattern
All the patterns in this section of the book are four squares across: these represent the four lettered holes in the tablet. The number of horizontal rows in the pattern indicates the number of tablets needed for that particular braid. Each of these patterns needs twelve tablets.

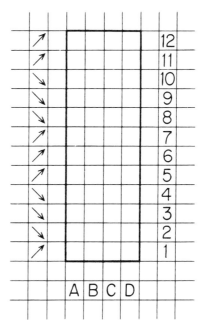

Direction of threading for this pattern

Number of tablets used in this pattern

The holes in each tablet

☐ light thread

☒ medium thread

■ dark thread

19

The arrow on the left of the pattern shows the direction in which all four threads must enter that tablet.

The filled-in squares represent the distribution of coloured threads in the tablets. Starting at the bottom of the 'Diamond' pattern, the first tablet should be threaded 'upwards', with a medium coloured thread through hole A, a light thread through hole B, a dark thread through

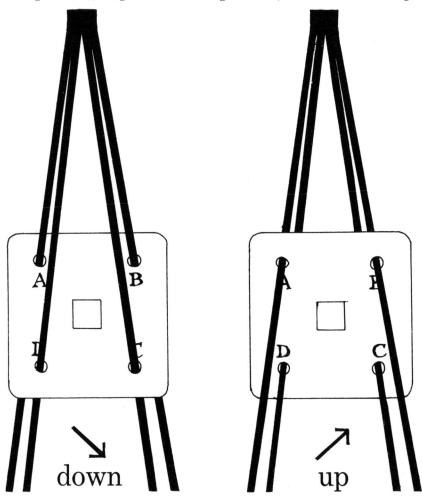

down

up

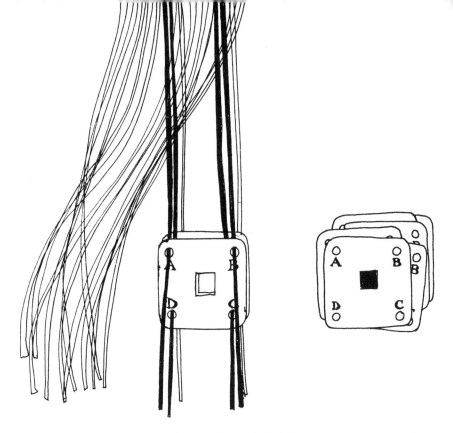

hole C, and another dark thread through hole D. The next row up gives the threading for the second tablet, this time threaded 'downwards' according to the arrow, and so on. (Be careful to note the order of lettering on the tablet, especially the positions of C and D.)

It is helpful to cover the pattern with a piece of card, and to slide this up row by row as the threading proceeds and as each tablet is dealt with.

Threading the tablets

A convenient way to work is to sit at a table facing the ends of the warp threads which are lying down its length. Have the correct number of tablets in a pile on the right (some weavers like to number them, temporarily, in pencil) and after threading each tablet according to the pattern, place it carefully on top of its predecessor in the centre, with A over A, etc. Try to disturb the warp as little as possible as the individual threads are selected otherwise it will become tangled. A way of preventing this is to tie a piece of thread tightly around the warp threads (in a bow so that undoing it will not involve the use of scissors

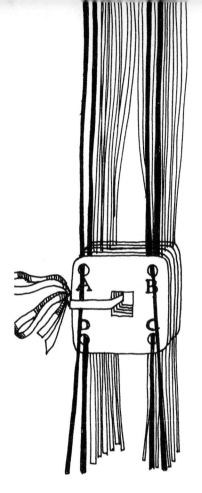

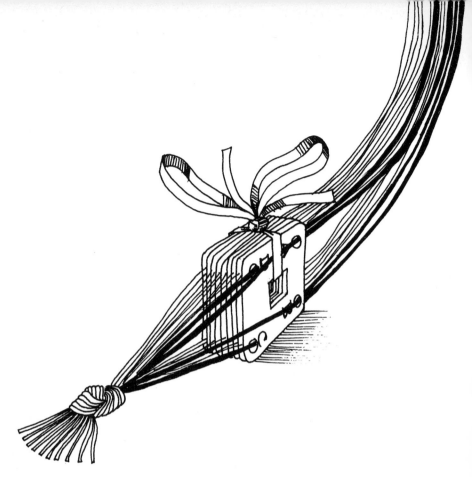

near the warp threads) about 380 mm (15 in.) from the end which is to be threaded. All tangles are thus kept the weaver's side of the bow.

Another method is to arrange the threads in groups of four, according to the pattern, before threading begins.

When the tablets are all threaded, tie a cord or tape of a contrasting colour through the centre hole (diagram left), or if there is no centre hole, around the pack like a parcel, both ways. This tape should tie the tablets firmly, so that they do not get out of place, but not tightly, so that the threads can move freely through the pack.

Preparing the weave
Stand the pack of tablets upright so that all the letters face to the right (diagram above). Tie a knot in each end of the warp, making sure that there are no slack threads.

Take the end furthest from the tablets and tie it firmly to something immovable: a tree, a doorknob, a radiator. Tie the other end to a length of strong thick string or tape and tie this to the back of a chair. Sit on the chair and move backwards until the warp is stretched very tightly.

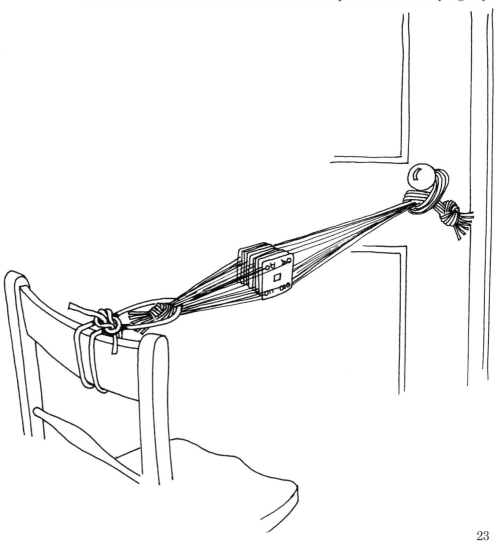

The weft

It is easier to make neat edges to the weaving if the weft is the same colour as the threads in the outside tablets wherever possible (tablets 1 and 12). Wind a few yards of this yarn around a piece of card, or make a dolly as described in the previous chapter.

Weaving

When the warp is tightly tensioned, and the weft is prepared, the safety tape around the tablets can be removed, but it must be replaced if it is necessary to leave the weaving at any time to prevent the tablets from getting out of position. An additional safety device would be to weave a string through every other set of 16 threads and back again, behind the tablets. Knot the ends together, and this prevents the tablets from jumping out of place. See diagram on page 60, *Luther Hooper's device*. The space between the top and bottom layers of threads is called the shed, and this is where the weft is put. A shed is already there, and can be used for the first weft shot. Pass the card or dolly through this opening, leaving a tail of weft hanging. Then, taking the pack of tablets in both hands, turn them away from you, allowing the threads to slip up between the tablets, until the next pair of letters is uppermost (C and D). Do not squeeze the tablets or hold them tensely, or turning will be difficult.

Pass the weft through the new shed. If it is difficult to find, run a finger down it from tablets to the near end or, taking the tablets together as a pack, slide them backwards and forwards a few times along the threads until the shed clears. Pull the weft thread gently but firmly into place so that it sits neatly against the selvedge. Beat it into place with the tapered edge of a ruler (this is sometimes easier to do when the next shed is formed). Continue in this way, turning the tablets one quarter turn away, for another three turns, inserting the weft each time.

The letters will now be back at their starting point (D and A uppermost). The next four turns are done *towards* the weaving. This completes one pattern repeat.

Most patterns in this book will be woven four away, four toward, in this way. If the tablets are twisted all in one direction a twist will build up behind the tablets which will restrict the weaving.

When a new length of weft thread is necessary, insert the new end so that it overlaps the old end by about 25 mm (1 in.), in the same shed.

Weave as far as the length of warp will allow, taking advantage of this sample warp to experiment with different degrees of beating: the pattern and texture will change considerably. When the braid is finished, give it a light press. If any difficulties occur when the work is in progress, see *How to correct faults*, page 28.

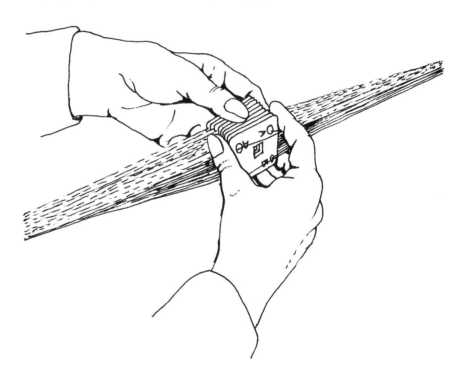

End treatments

At the end of any piece of tablet woven braid, it is usually necessary to secure the weft firmly so that it does not unravel. At its simplest, this will mean threading the weft through a needle and darning it back through the weaving in the shed of the previous weft shot, leaving the

a

b

26

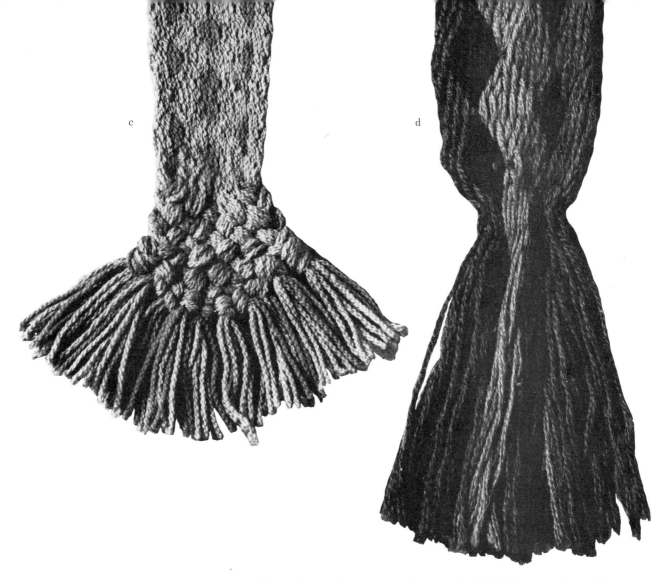

c

d

cut fringe. Sometimes a more decorative finish is wanted, and here are four different treatments.

(a) This was dictated by the nature of the pattern of the braid: three separate shuttles were used for the last few inches.

(b) Whipping the top inch of each bunch of warp threads.

(c) Dividing and plaiting, finishing with overhand knots.

(d) The last few weft shots were pulled tightly before being secured with a needle.

How to correct faults

(a) If the pattern fails to appear correctly after weaving for an inch or two.

1 Look at the under surface of the braid: the pattern may be correct but the braid is being woven upside-down.

2 Check the point at which the tablets are being reversed. By changing this point the pattern may correct itself.

3 Check the lettering on the tablets: all the A's must be at the same corner of the pack at the start. It may be necessary later for some types of patterning to turn the tablets individually, but no card should be out of place at the start of weaving. If it is, turn it away or towards, usually only one quarter-turn, to correct its position.

4 Check that the tablets are all facing the same way, and check that they are threaded in the right directions (up or down). If one is wrong, isolate that group of four threads, tie up the pack of tablets on each side to keep them in order when the tension is slackened, and slip the tablet to the back of the warp. It is then possible to untie the whole warp at the far end, and slip off the incorrect tablet, re-placing it correctly. Alternatively the four threads can be withdrawn from the weaving at the front and tied back in with the rest of the warp after correction. They will begin to weave in as the work progresses. The tension of these four threads must be checked and made equal to the rest of the work after the disturbance, however.

(b) Uneven selvedges.

1 Make sure that the weft thread is the same colour as the edge threads of the warp wherever possible, as this helps to disguise any unevenness.

2 If loops of weft appear at the edge, try to pull the weft a little more snugly against the selvedge threads before beating it into position. If the weft thread is pulled too tightly, however, the edge threads will strain inwards and eventually break, so it is essential to develop a technique of placing just the right tension on the weft thread.

(c) Uneven pattern, caused by uneven beating. When starting to weave it is necessary to concentrate on inserting a regular number of weft threads per 25 mm (1 in.). Later this will become automatic if care is

opposite Examples of lettering (see page 80) and Egyptian diagonal pattern (see page 82)

28

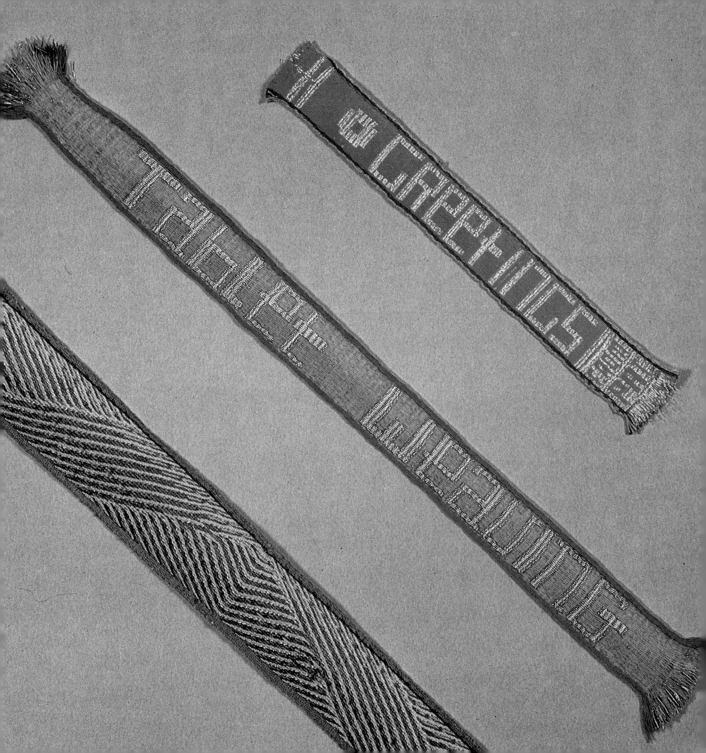

taken at the beginning. Sometimes even taking a coffee break can show in the difference in beat in weaving, and any pattern will be affected by this difference.

(d) Unpicking. It is possible to reverse the turning process and remove weft in order to get back to the point of a mistake, but it is not easy. Try to avoid distractions when doing it. One difficulty is that most threads will bind together with fluff during unpicking, and all this fluff must be removed with care before unpicking can continue. Any fluff remaining when starting to weave again will show in a line across the braid.

(e) Slack warp threads. One or more slack warp threads must be tightened up to the tension of the rest, or they will cause mistakes and look unsightly. Pull the offending thread back through the weaving towards the weaver, with the help of a pin, then use the pin to secure it at the beginning of the weaving.

(f) Difficult shed. Sometimes the yarn used proves to be unsuitable for tablet weaving and tends to fluff and cling together, making the shed indistinct. An emergency measure which sometimes works, especially on wool, is to paint olive oil, or a good cooking oil, on to the warp threads. After weaving the braid must, of course, be washed carefully in warm soapy water.

(g) Broken thread. This can be mended by taking about 1 m ($3\frac{1}{4}$ ft) of the same yarn and tying it to the broken end at the back of the warp *without shortening the old end,* with a firm bow, as far away from the tablets as possible. Bring the new end through the appropriate tablet, and push a pin into the woven braid. Wind the near end of the new length around the pin in a figure-of-eight, making sure that the tension is the same as the rest of the warp. As weaving progresses, the bow will move nearer to the tablets, and eventually it can be undone, when the original end will be found to be long enough to bring through the tablet in place of the new piece, pinning and checking tension as before. All ends can be darned in later. See diagram overleaf.

Mending a broken thread (see previous page). (The rest of the tablets have been omitted from the diagram for the sake of clarity)

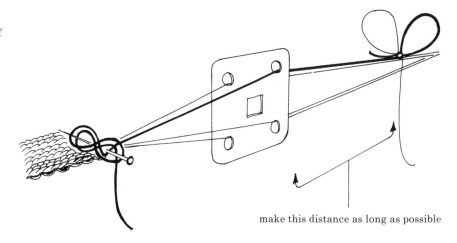

make this distance as long as possible

Patterns for braids using up to twenty tablets

On the next few pages are photographs and drafts (working plans) for braids which are all possible using the minimum equipment described in a previous chapter. Any one of these patterns can be used to make the small items (tie, watchstrap, sash, etc.) suggested on pages 44 to 48. They can also be joined side-by-side to make some of the articles which are suggested for wider braids in Part Two.

All the patterns in this section have been designed to be woven with the 'four quarter turns away, four towards' system of working. It is worthwhile trying out other turning systems on any spare warp, however.

Counterchange
17 tablets
2 colours

Ripple
16 tablets
2 colours

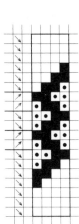

Lizard
19 tablets
3 colours

Tigerstripe
17 tablets
2 colours

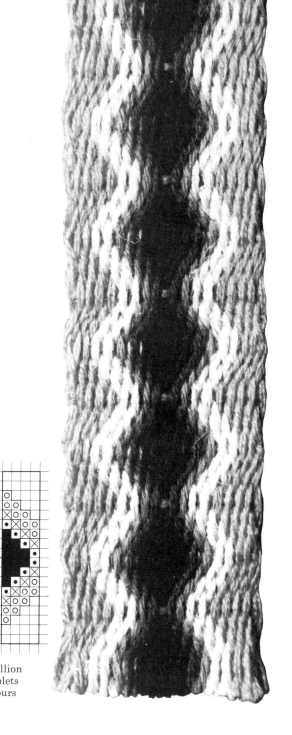

Medallion
18 tablets
5 colours

Ogee
18 tablets
4 colours

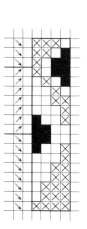

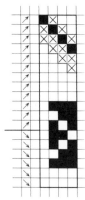

Cross
18 tablets
3 colours

Poppy
18 tablets
3 colours

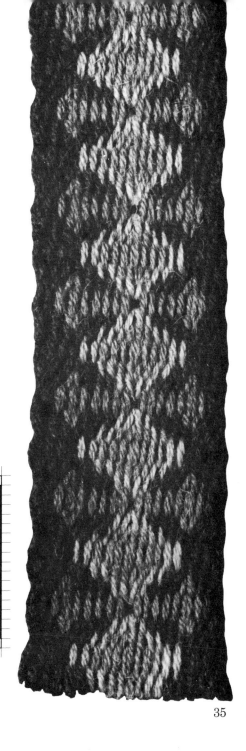

Snakeskin
16 tablets
2 colours

Apple
18 tablets
4 colours

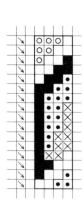

Small arrow
16 tablets
5 colours

36

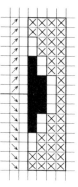

Small circle
16 tablets
3 colours

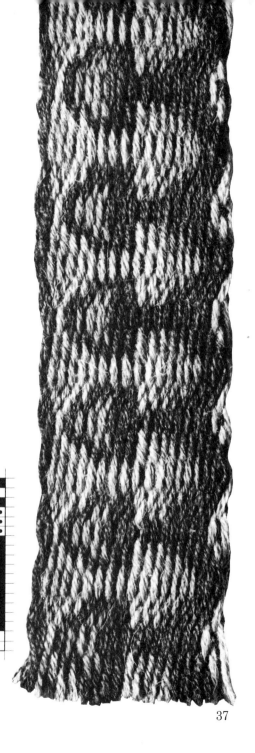

Zig-zag
16 tablets
4 colours

Bud
18 tablets
4 colours

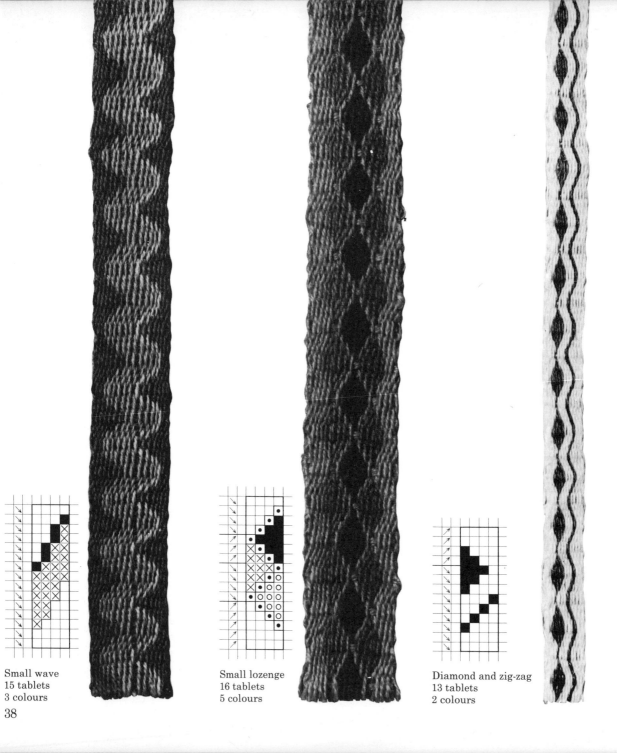

Small wave
15 tablets
3 colours

Small lozenge
16 tablets
5 colours

Diamond and zig-zag
13 tablets
2 colours

Reversals

Although most of the patterns for braids in this book are of the 'four quarter-turns away, four towards' type, it is, of course, possible to weave any of them (with a different result) by turning the tablets in one direction only until the point comes where the build-up of twist at the far end of the warp begins to hinder progress. By reversing the direction of the turning now, this can be undone again during the weaving, but the pattern is reversed at that point. This point of reversal can be made into a design feature, and many braids with definite numbers of 'away' and 'towards' turns can be planned which will avoid the problem of twisting altogether.

The illustrations show the different effects which can be obtained on the same warp and threading, merely by altering the number of turns before reversing.

Alternatively, a solution for the build-up of twist, which is inevitable when turning in one direction, is to have two weavers, one at each end of the warp, one set of cards in the middle, producing two lengths of braid at the same time.

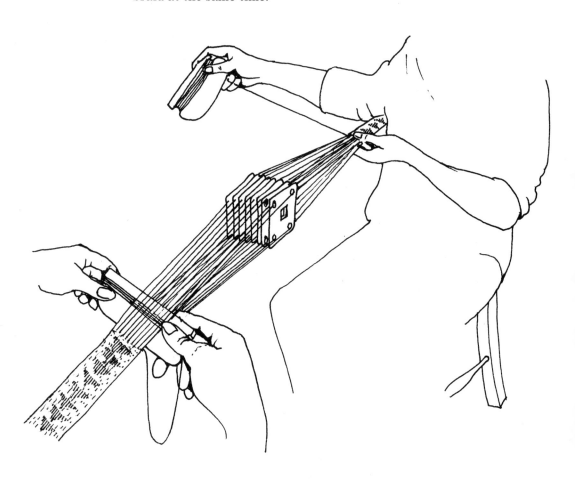

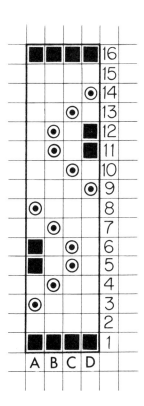

How to design

It is possible to design a braid consisting of parts of existing patterns: some of the wider braids in Part Two are amalgamations of two or more narrow braids or of parts of patterns shown in Part One. However, it is also interesting to design an original braid.

When starting to design, it is easier to design and weave samples with no specific use or width in mind. At the end of the chapter there are directions for designing braids for specific uses.

Stage one   Take some graph paper or rule out a grid measuring four squares wide and any number of squares (representing a convenient number of tablets) long. Fill this space with any pattern, using symbols or coloured pens to indicate areas of different coloured threads.

See, for example, the draft on the left.

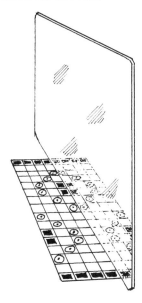

Bear in mind that where the design touches the edge of the area it will repeat itself in a mirror-like way, if the normal practice of reversing after every four turns is followed. A small hand-mirror held to the edge will show what the pattern will look like when woven.

Stage two Now the direction of threading of each tablet must be determined. This is a very important stage of designing, as the design will depend on the clarity of its lines, and if no notice is taken of the threading direction, jagged lines will result in some parts.

There are two rules to follow:

(a) When a diagonal line on the design slopes up from left to right then the tablets must be threaded downwards (mark ↘ by the row in question).

(b) When a diagonal slopes up from right to left then the tablets must be threaded upwards (mark ↗ by the row).

This will produce a smooth line in the pattern.

If this rule is disregarded, some lines will be jagged. See opposite.

The pattern which was started in stage one will now look like this:

Right

In theory, it would not matter in which direction tablets 1, 2, 15 and 16 were threaded. But in practice it will be found that reversing the direction at the edge helps to make a firmer braid. If the diagonals run to the edge anyway, then there will be no question of the direction changing.

Colour It will be found that contrasting tones are most effective and make accurate weaving easier; close tones do not show up the pattern to advantage. A general rule would be to use a more definite change of hue and tone than one might choose for other types of work. Trying to be subtle usually results in a patternless braid.

Designing for a purpose Remember that the beating up of the weft will affect the braid's qualities. If the article to be woven has to tie loosely and hang well, then few weft threads per inch would give this quality. If the braid is to be hard-wearing then the weft must be beaten up more firmly. Any pattern will expand or contract in length accordingly, of course.

Width This is decided by weaving a braid in the same yarn, and measuring how many tablets are needed per 25 mm (1 in.). There is no other safe way to calculate accurately. A small difference in width measurement can be made in the way in which the cards are held and the weft pulled into position.

Length As a general rule, add 15 per cent extra warp to the length of braid required (to allow for the twisting of the thread) and also add 1 m ($3\frac{1}{4}$ ft) to allow for the knots and the piece of warp wasted at the end of each warp. As this metre applies only once to each warp, it is therefore economical to thread up as long a warp as is practicable.

Wrong

Here are some suggestions for items which a beginner can make using any pattern.

Ties

Because a tie must hang well and not twist, it is important that the weft is beaten into position only lightly. Almost any width is possible, and the narrowed part which fits around the neck is achieved simply by pulling the weft thread in more tightly at that point, allowing the warp to ease back to its original width again to complete the tie.

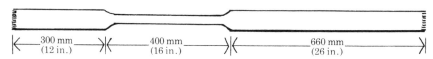

|←——300 mm——→|←——400 mm——→|←——660 mm——→|
| (12 in.) | (16 in.) | (26 in.) |

Sash belt
Obviously, this can be woven to any length, and the ends finished in many different ways. The one in the photograph is 1·2 m (4 ft) long, and to finish off the ends the first and last shots of weft were pulled in tightly before being secured.

uses for tablet weaving

choker has long fringed ends threaded with beads.

Open welt threads give decorative 'slashed' sleeve look.

Overskirt strips sewn on to waistband, allowed to flare loose over underskirt.

Long knitted dress has braid around armholes, crosses over at the centre back, then comes to tie in the front

Knitted tank top with woven straps + neckline.

Liven-up sandles with colourful braid.

WALL POCKET

Decorative +
functional,
wall pocket

Tabard, vertical
strips sewn together,
end pieces tie under
arms.

Poncho, leave ends
of vertical strips
as fringes for
hemline

Braid
around
the edge
of a jacket.
Woven belt,
held by rouleau-
looped buttons.

Shoulder bag.
Narrow band
becoming wider,
turned over to
form a pocket.
End with knots
+ fringing.

Horizontal strips
sewn together, to
make interesting
hemline of skirt.
Or as a cuff to pants.

Watch straps

Materials must be chosen carefully to withstand surface friction. Mercerised cotton or linen threads should be suitable. The weft can be beaten more firmly than for the previous two items, because a hard-wearing, non-draping braid is needed.

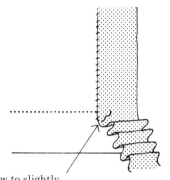

sew to slightly
below dotted line

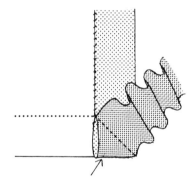

if the braid is bulky
it may be necessary
to cut off this triangle

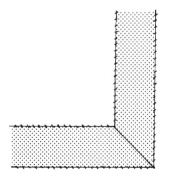

How to apply braids and fringes

A common use for tablet weaving is in the form of braids which are then sewn on to items of dress or furnishing. When preparing the design for this type of application, many things must be taken into consideration if the combination of braid and fabric is to be successful. The braid must also be sewn on very neatly if the care taken in weaving the braid is not to be wasted.

Care in choosing the colours and type of pattern is necessary. It is good practice to try placing any samples of braid on different types of fabric, and to try to work out why some pairings look better than others.

Weight is important. A thick wool braid will look well with a woollen cloth (flannel, tweed, felt, etc) or with leather, velvet or fur, but will often be too heavy for a lighter fabric.

The braid lines on the fabric should be planned so that curves are avoided as much as possible and corners are square; tablet woven braids are comparatively inflexible.

In order to calculate the length required, pin a length of tape to the fabric, remove and measure. Allow extra for mitring corners and finishing ends.

If the ends of the braid are to be caught into the seam of a garment for neatness, it will be necessary to sew the braid to the fabric before the garment is made up. Small areas like pockets may be easier to handle if braid is attached before joining to the rest of the garment.

Hand stitching with small, neat stitches catching regularly into the weft loops at the edges of the braid is by far the best method of attaching it.

It is always essential to measure the positioning of the braid and to mark often, using tailor's chalk or thread, not pins because they tend to slope unless inserted very carefully.

A braid over 38 mm (1½ in.) wide will need more rows of stitching than a narrower braid. A row or two down the centre can prevent a wide braid from bagging outwards in use.

Always find an inconspicuous place to begin and end the braid.

When taking braid around a corner, a mitre is essential to give a neat finish. If the braid is bulky it may be necessary to cut it, but finer ones can often be folded neatly, leaving the length complete.

Braid can be applied neatly around a slit, or to give the appearance of a slit.

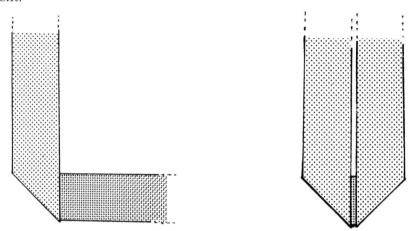

A square mitre can then be produced by folding back the point.

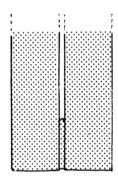

This form of working the braid around a slit is suitable for tablet weaving because the reverse side is never seen.

Press and tack the braid into these forms before applying it; it will then be easier to sew on.

When attaching tablet weaving by hand, be careful not to pull the sewing thread too tight, or puckering will occur. If sewing by machine, keep both the braid and the fabric taut.

To apply a fringe and finish the edge of the fabric at the same time, place the wrong side of the fringe to the wrong side of the fabric, with the lower edge of the heading 7 mm ($\frac{1}{4}$ in.) from the edge of the fabric. Stitch along that edge, turn fringe to right side and press, then stitch along top edge of heading.

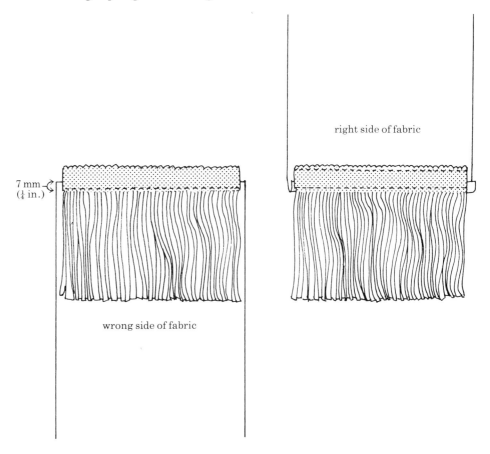

right side of fabric

7 mm
($\frac{1}{4}$ in.)

wrong side of fabric

Braid trimming around lampshades, wall-coverings, notice-boards, etc can be stuck on, using *Copydex* according to the manufacturer's instructions, mitring corners as if stitching.

Part two

A loom specifically designed for tablet weaving which can be made with a few simple tools. The bar at the far (right hand side in the diagram) end is not fixed: the warp is wound around it in a figure-of-eight, secured with a half hitch, and then attached temporarily to one of the front three bars. The tablets are suspended on the warp. When a short length of braid has been woven, the warp can be tensioned by threading the braid in an over-under fashion through the three bars, and then back again towards the tablets, like a friction buckle

Up to this point the techniques and patterns shown have been suitable for a non-weaver beginner. The second half of this book contains descriptions of techniques and patterns for wider braids. Some of these are impracticable without some more elaborate equipment than that suggested for Part One, if possible a simple loom. It is a good idea to have some experience of tablet weaving before attempting any of the techniques that follow.

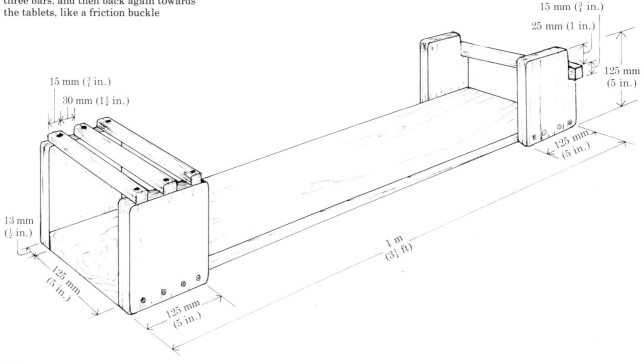

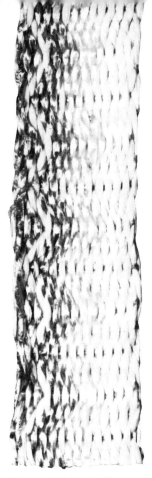

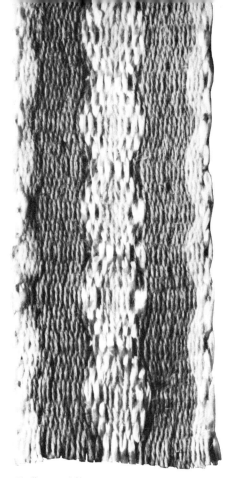

Matt and shiny *Raffene* *Raffene* and linen Wool and chenille

Materials

More adventurous use of materials becomes possible once the basic technique has been mastered. Narrow ribbon (7 mm ($\frac{1}{4}$ in.) ribbon in red and green is sold in stationers shops for tying up documents), chenille, metal threads, fine threads such as *Sylko*, brushed mohair (too much will get tangled up, but a few strands can be included), space-dyed yarns, linens, and jute, hemp and polypropylene strings and twines of all types, plastic threads; all these can be used, as can any material which is strong enough to withstand the strain of weaving and smooth enough to provide a shed free from fluff. Thicker yarns, such as rug-wool, can be used but will need larger tablets.

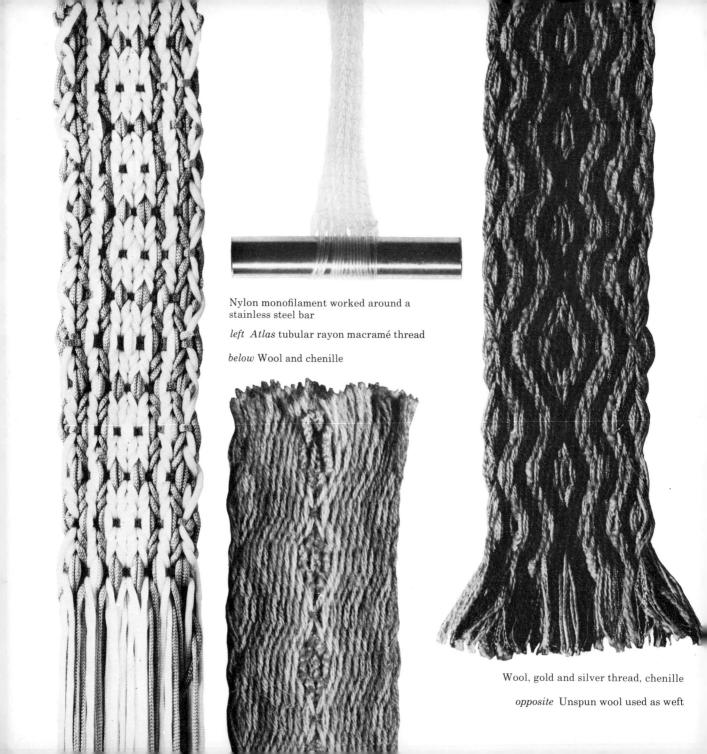

Nylon monofilament worked around a stainless steel bar

left *Atlas* tubular rayon macramé thread

below Wool and chenille

Wool, gold and silver thread, chenille

opposite Unspun wool used as weft

Other ways to prepare a warp

Not surprisingly with a technique which has been practised over most parts of the world for thousands of years, there are many different ways of warping and threading the tablets.

The simple way described in Part One, suitable for beginners, can be speeded up by using a weaver's warping equipment.

If a spool-rack is available, or a substitute can be improvised, then this method used by tablet weavers in Morocco is possible. The stand and the weaving-board can also be improvised (see diagrams below and on page 52), but the warping-board is standard weaver's equipment.

For a two colour warp, place four spools of each colour on the rack. Thread the first tablet with four ends from the spools—colours accord-

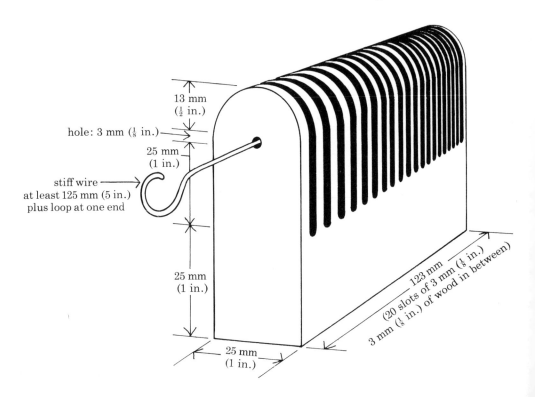

ing to pattern. Place the tablet in a stand, securing it with a wire pushed through the centre, and then warp the required length between the pegs of a warping-board (in Morocco this would be 5·5 m (6 yd)), cutting the threads at the end and tying them to the far post. Repeat with the next tablet. When all the tablets are threaded, then the warp is wound from the far end on to a short stick (usually a 150 mm (6 in.) length of thick bamboo) in a figure-of-eight movement. When winding is complete, a hitch secures the warp to the stick and it is lodged behind a notch at one end of a weaving-board, more warp being released from time-to-time as weaving progresses. This could also be a useful method of handling a longer warp when using the doorknob-to-chair way of working.

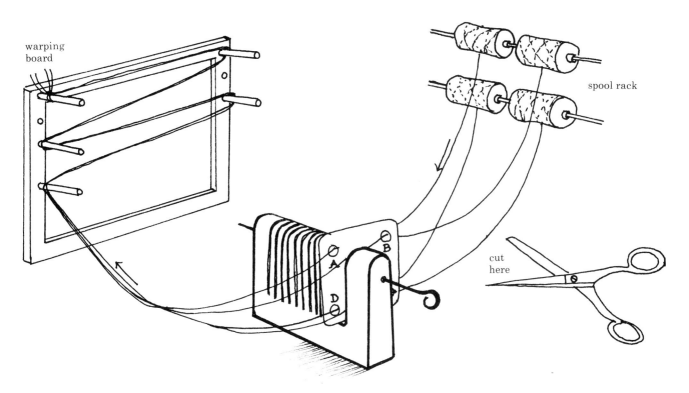

warping board

spool rack

cut here

In Morocco, the tablet stand becomes a warp spreader during weaving, hanging from the warp with a group of four threads in each slot, passing under the wire.

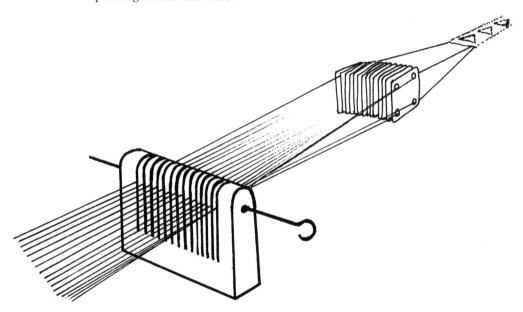

Another way of threading-up (definitely not for beginners) for a two colour warp (say black and white) place four spools of each colour on a spool rack. Clamp two posts so that they stick out, not up, from a table, the necessary length apart (ie the length of the warp). Thread *all* the tablets with black threads, and warp backwards and forwards for as many times as there are all-black tablets shown in the whole pattern, dropping a tablet off each time near the first post. Then cut one black thread and tie in a white one in its place, and warp as many three black one white tablets as indicated in the draft, again dropping a tablet off the pile each time, and placing these tablets in the right places in relation to the all-black ones. When the correct number of three black one white tablets, have been warped, repeat the process with two black two white tablets, and so on, until all tablets are warped and in their right place. Check that they face the right direction (the equivalent of being threaded up and down) by 'flipping' if necessary, and it may also be necessary to turn the occasional tablet one quarter-turn to place it correctly. Tie through the tablets to secure them, tie the warp at each end and slide off the pegs.

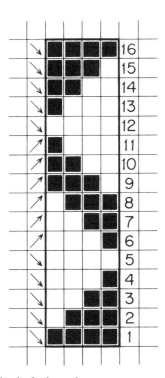

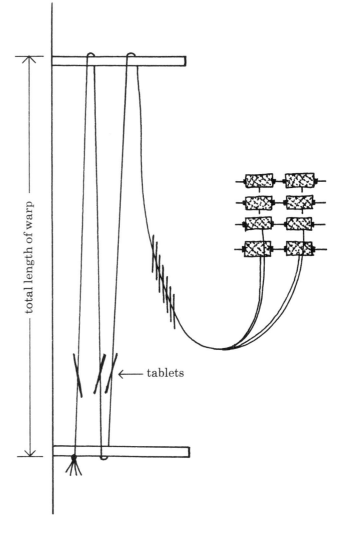

In the draft above there are
2 tablets threaded with 4 black threads (1 and 16)
4 tablets threaded with 3 black, 1 white threads (2, 8, 9, 15)
4 tablets threaded with 2 black, 2 white threads (3, 7, 10, 14)
4 tablets threaded with 1 black, 3 white threads (4, 6, 11, 13)
2 tablets threaded with 4 white threads (5 and 12)

Luther Hooper's device

An interesting device for avoiding the build-up of twist is described in Luther Hooper's book *Weaving with Small Appliances: Tablet Weaving* (Pitman). In this system the warp is weighted at the far end, not attached to a fixed point. A small raddle, or row of nails, is fixed at the far point, and each group of four threads is placed in a dent or space. A fishing weight, or other lead weight, is attached to the end of each group, which is then free to spin round as necessary. In this way patterns can be woven with the tablets being turned in one direction for the whole length of the braid.

safety device which can be used on any warp

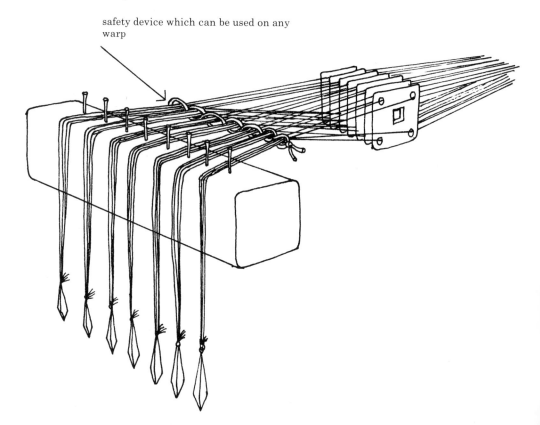

opposite Skirt with bands of tablet weaving (see page 101)

Weaving with 2, 3, 5, 6 hole tablets

Tablet woven braids may be woven with two holes only (use two diagonally opposite ones on a four hole tablet), three holes in a triangular tablet, five holes in a pentagon, six holes in a hexagon. The patterns can be worked out over the appropriate number of squares of graph paper. As each 'cord' is composed of the number of threads in the tablet, it is obvious that as the number increases so the cord gets thicker and stronger. Curiously, though, there is little obvious pattern difference, although there is scope for more elaborate designs and colourings. With the larger numbers, yarns must be chosen carefully so that they have no fibres projecting. With some tablets more than one weaving position is possible, and sometimes more than one shed is available.

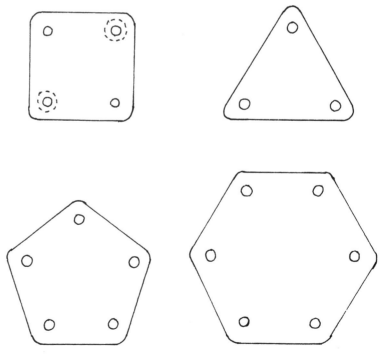

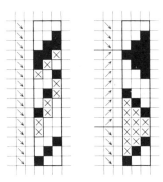

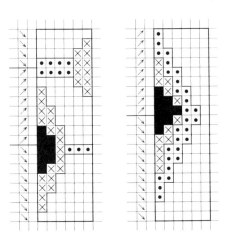

above 2 designs for 3 hole tablets
right 2 designs for 6 hole tablets

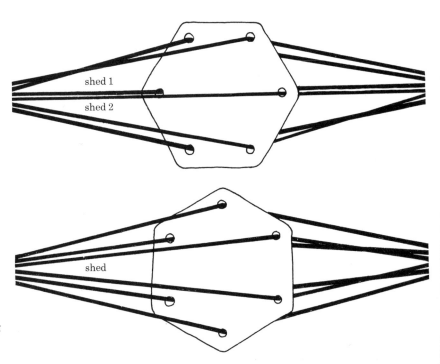

shed 1

shed 2

shed

With some tablets more than one weaving
position is possible, and sometimes more
than one shed is available

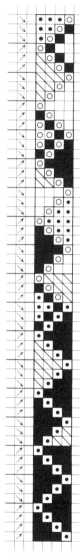

Shaded diamond
55 tablets
5 colours

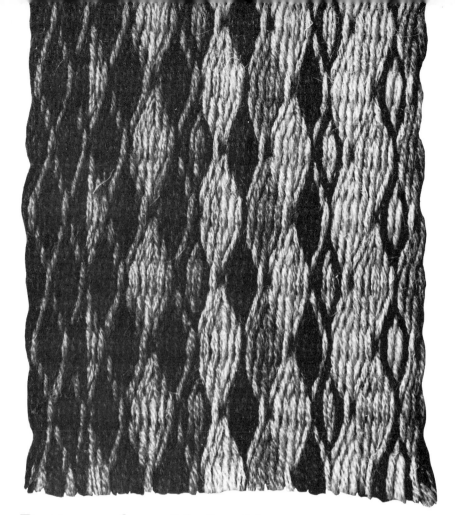

Patterns for wide braids

Braids of more than about 50 mm (2 in.) wide are easier to weave if some sort of warp spreader is used. This can take the form of a small piece of reed (the type used in ordinary weaving) either fixed or hanging from the warp, or the type of tablet-stand-cum-reed as used in North Africa (see page 58).

If a loom is available, the reed can be used in its normal position. If necessary, two or more weavers can work at one wide loom, by mounting several warps side-by-side, allowing 457 mm (18 in.) between each, removing the shafts and fixing a reed towards the back of the loom.

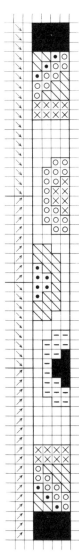

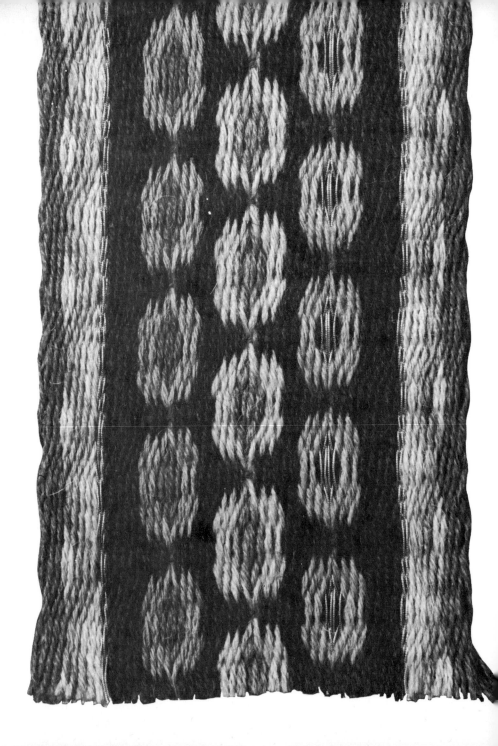

Three flowers
54 tablets
7 colours

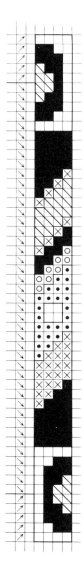

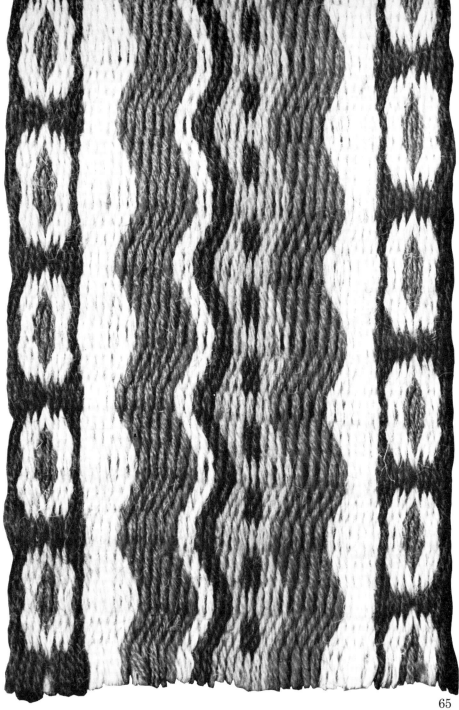

Zig-zag and flowers
53 tablets
6 colours

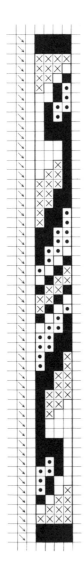

River
53 tablets
4 colours

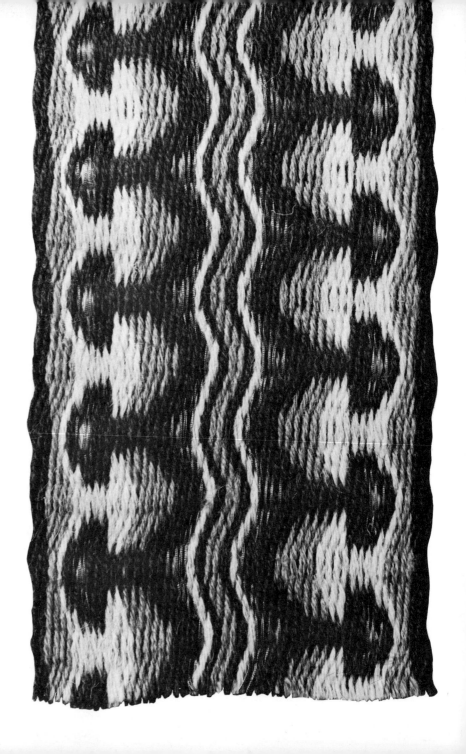

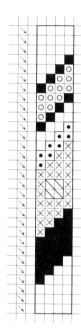

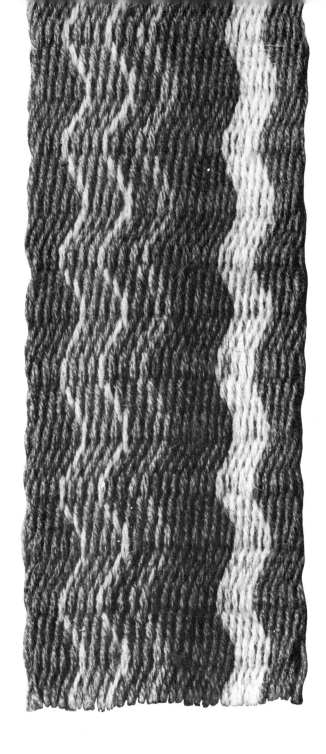

Spotted zig-zag
30 cards
6 colours

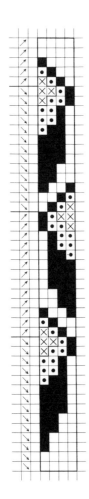

Almond
45 tablets
4 colours

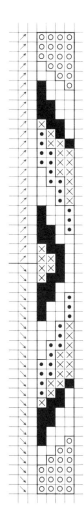

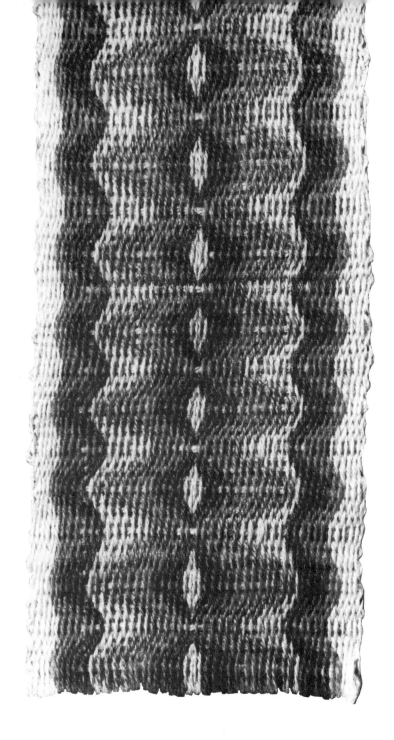

Strawberry
48 tablets
5 colours

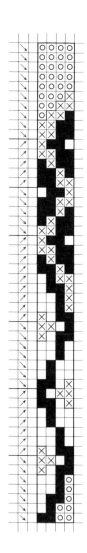

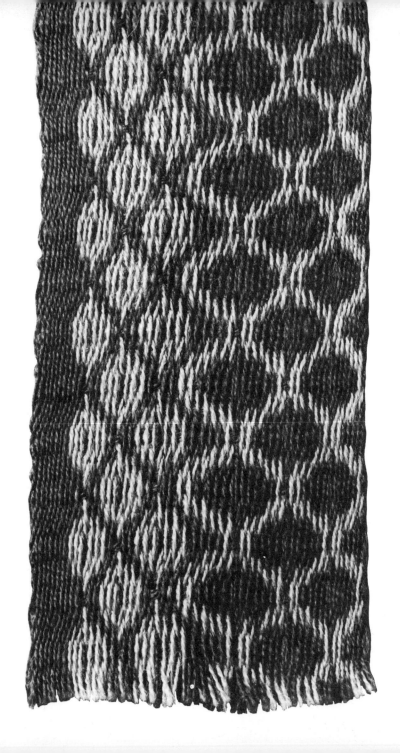

Python
50 tablets
4 colours

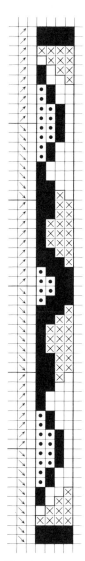

Hands
54 tablets
4 colours

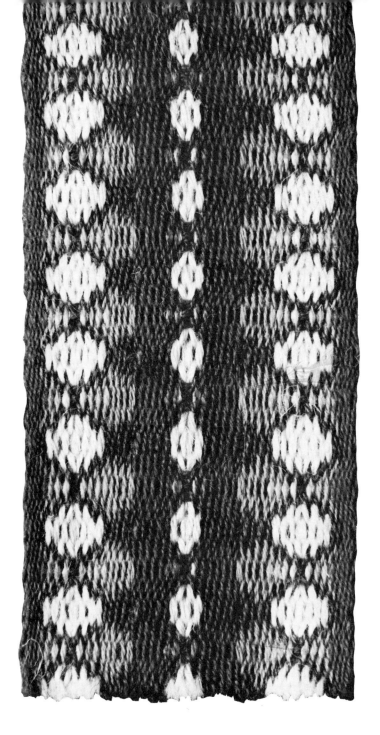

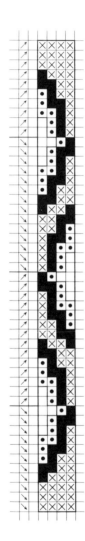

Target
49 tablets
4 colours

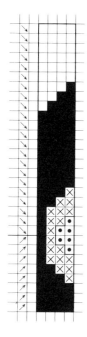

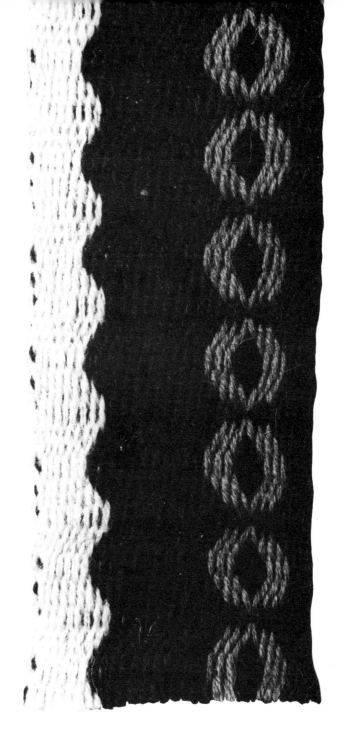

Flower and wave
30 tablets
4 colours

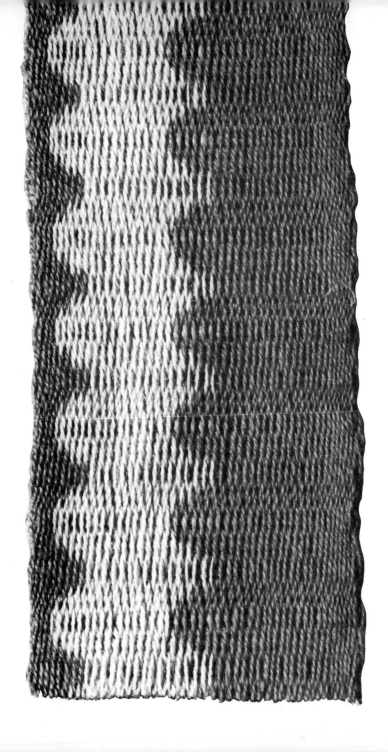

Simple zig-zag
47 tablets
3 colours

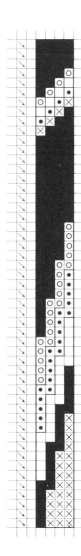

Rainbow
51 tablets
5 colours

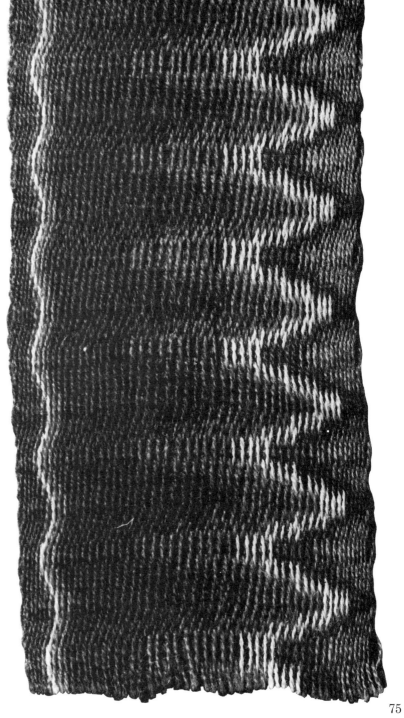

Variations on one warp

In Part One of this book patterned braids were obtained by threading the tablets from a draft and turning them in a simple rhythm. An alternative is to thread them with a simple colour system and then to arrange the tablets before weaving each piece. In this way many different patterns can be woven on the same warp without re-threading.

All the braids shown in this chapter were woven on one warp: 27 tablets threaded with two colours, colour 1 in holes A and B, and colour 2 in holes C and D.

(a) A simple reversible braid is possible, showing all colour 1 on one side, and colour 2 on the other.
  1 Put the weft across in the existing shed. (D and A should be uppermost.)
  2 Turn the tablets one quarter-turn towards.
  3 Weft across.
  4 Tablets one quarter-turn away.
  5 Weft across.
  6 Tablets one quarter-turn away.
  7 Weft across.
  8 Tablets one quarter-turn towards.
  9 Weft across.
10 Tablets one quarter-turn towards.
Repeat steps 3 to 10.

To change the colours from one face to the other: when the tablets are back to their original position, turn them two quarter-turns away, then two quarter-turns towards, inserting a weft shot at each turn, and continue in this way.

(b) A reversible striped braid can be woven in the same way. With the tablets in their original position, take the nine tablets in the middle and turn them two quarter-turns away before starting to weave. Then weave as for the previous braid. Many variations are possible in reversible stripes, and these can be made into checks by following the colour-change procedure in braid (a).

a

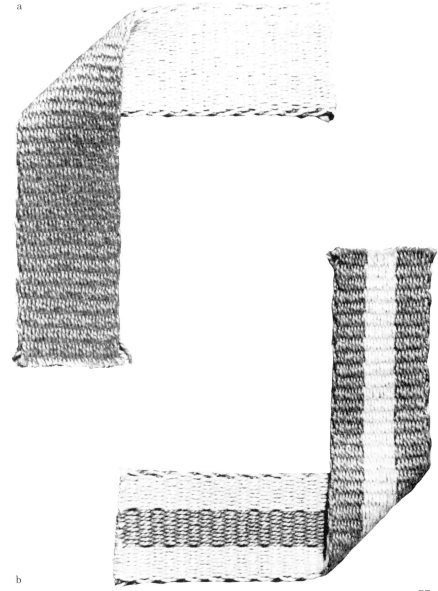

b

c

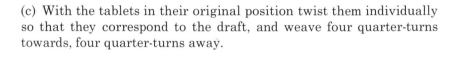

(c) With the tablets in their original position twist them individually so that they correspond to the draft, and weave four quarter-turns towards, four quarter-turns away.

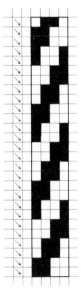

4 turns
each way

The four braids on the opposite page all rely on some of the tablets being flipped around before weaving, as if some of them had been threaded up and some down. The tablets have also been twisted to give a colour arrangement. Details are shown on the drafts.

All turned the same way

4 turns
each way

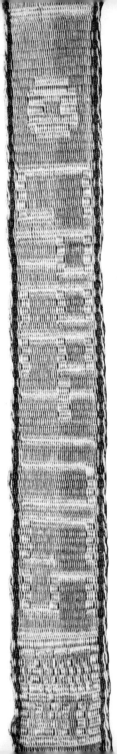

Lettering

Lettering is not easy, but the principles involved are useful to master as any design can then be produced. Use a cotton warp to begin with, so that turning and any undoing is easier.

Thread up the tablets as for *Variations on one warp,* page 76. (Holes A and B: colour 1; holes C and D: colour 2.)

It is essential to draw out the required lettering before beginning to weave. When planning out the letters and spacings needed, it must be remembered that the thinnest horizontal (across the warp) line possible is usually equal to two tablets' width vertically on the plan. So, to weave a square, the graph-paper must show a rectangle twice as wide as it is long.

First, do a few inches as background, with all colour 1 showing:

Weft 1 Holes A and B uppermost (all colour 1).

Weft 2 Turn all tablets one quarter-turn away until D and A are uppermost (half colour 1, half colour 2).

Weft 3 Turn all tablets towards so that A and B are up again (all colour 1).

Weft 4 Turn tablets towards again, so that holes B and C are uppermost (half colour 1, half colour 2).

Continue in this way, two quarter-turns towards, two away, until ready to start the lettering. The sequence must end with half colour 1, half colour 2, uppermost (either *weft 2* or *weft 4*). Then, reading from the squared paper, count the tablets, pushing the background ones into one group, and the lettering ones into another group further up the warp.

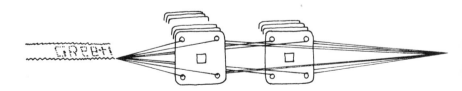

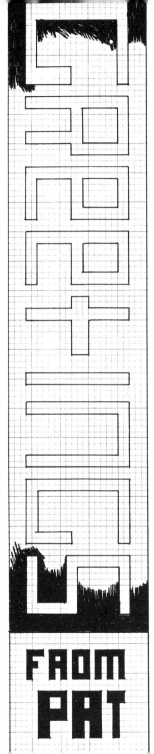

These two groups continue to turn two quarter-turns towards, and two away, but *always in opposite directions*. For instance, if holes D and A were up to start with, then the background group would turn *away* so that all colour 1 is up, and the lettering group will turn *towards* so that all colour 2 is up. Both groups will turn a second time, the background group away again and the figuring group towards.

At this point the groups can be altered according to the next row on the pattern, ie background tablets can join the figuring or vice versa.

The tablets must only move from one group to another when both groups have half colour 1 and half colour 2 up, never when the solid colours are up.

It is easy, when a beginner, to forget which way the tablets are turning. The rule is:

If half colour 1 and half colour 2 are up, then the tablets obviously have to turn in the direction which will bring up the correct solid colour.

If solid colours are up, look at the weaving and decide which warp threads are due to go down.

Plan for lettering in the photograph., showing the counterchange of colours at the end. The original was woven in *Sylko* and fine round metal thread

Egyptian diagonal pattern

This too can be woven on the warp prepared for *Variations on one warp*, page 76. Turn the cards round individually so that the colours are arranged like this:

Turn all cards away for four quarter-turns. Then at the right hand side, slide two cards forward in the warp and turn them a quarter-turn towards. Turn the main pack a quarter-turn away. Put weft across and repeat. Slide the next two cards forward, and repeat the turning. Continue like this until all the cards are together in the front pack. Make two quarter-turns towards with the whole pack (weft between each turn), then repeat the whole process starting on the left hand side, now turning the main pack towards and the rest away. See colour plate facing page 28.

Many variations on this technique will suggest themselves. In the photograph opposite, several bands of Egyptian pattern share the same weft. See page 85.

Braids sharing the same weft

A loom is essential for this type of fabric-making with tablet weaving. It is also necessary to select a weft thread which is soft and non-slippery, or textured, so that the warp threads are unable to slide into the gaps. A long stick shuttle, a few inches longer than the width of the fabric, helps the beating to be consistent on all the bands. See opposite.

Warp becomes weft

One tablet-full of threads passes through the shed after a number of turns. No other weft is used. This is a traditional method for making animal halters in Greece. The tablet which is to be weft as well as warp is secured separately at the far end. After all the tablets have been turned a number of times, take the weft tablet and put it through the shed, where it will lodge itself; then release the ends at the far point. These ends are then drawn through behind the tablet and fixed again at the far end and the process is repeated.

Spaced warp

A reed is essential for this: the groups of four threads are spaced 7 mm ($\frac{1}{4}$ in.) apart in the reed, and threaded through the tablets alternately up and down, so that they prop each other up during weaving. A wider fabric would be possible if the tablets were turned in groups rather than all at once.

Beads

Two shuttles are used when weaving with beads, one as a 'binder' weft, the other carrying the beads, threaded in order, which can then be dropped off where needed. The 'binder' weft holds the braid neatly together even when loops of beads are being dropped at the edge of a braid. The shuttle with the beads can be taken through every other shed, alternating with the binder.

To thread the beads on to the weft, roll the end of the thread in quick-drying glue, and it will then act as a needle.

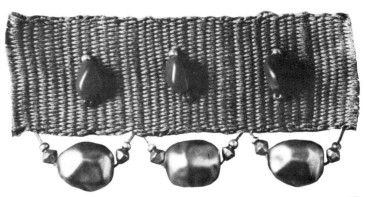

Fringe and picot edges

Two wefts are useful in this type of weaving: one to form the fringe or loops, and another 'binder' thread to stop the warp threads from wandering at the edge. A wooden gauge—a ruler or a pencil—is useful when making a looped fringe or picot. As for tablet weaving with beads, the wefts are taken through every other shed, alternating with each other.

A quick way to weave a cut fringe would be to set up two warps on a loom with a space between, sharing a weft which would later be cut up the middle.

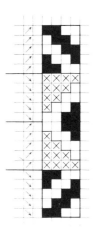

Braids with corded edges

The tablets on each edge are turned with the central ones, but the weft is passed across the central area only, leaving the edges to twist and form cords. These are woven into the main body of the braid again at some point before the reversal of the pattern and released again the same distance after, so that they do not untwist with the change of direction in the cord-turning.

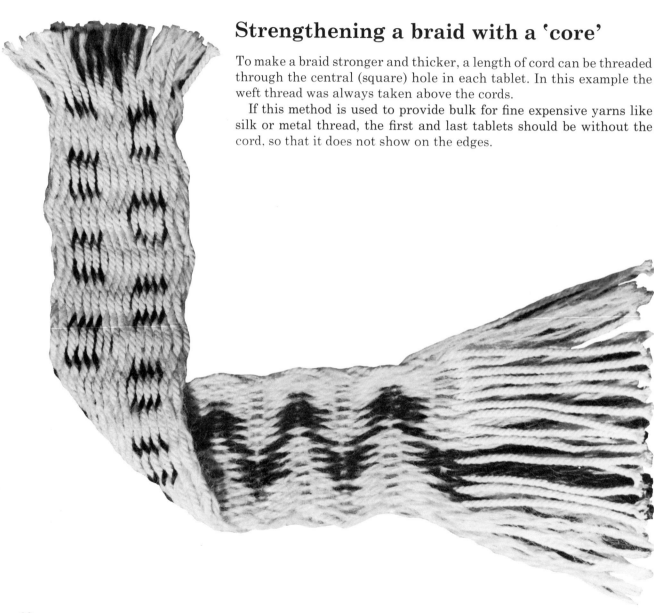

Strengthening a braid with a 'core'

To make a braid stronger and thicker, a length of cord can be threaded through the central (square) hole in each tablet. In this example the weft thread was always taken above the cords.

If this method is used to provide bulk for fine expensive yarns like silk or metal thread, the first and last tablets should be without the cord, so that it does not show on the edges.

Tubular weaving

Here are two ways of weaving a tube with tablets:

(a) Put the weft across from one side only, pulling it tightly across the back of the braid. When it is woven and off the loom, slip a dowel up inside the tube and slide the warp threads around until they meet on the other side. Tube and flat weaving can be combined.

(b) Another way is to use both the sheds which are apparent when the tablets are standing on one corner rather than the usual flat base.

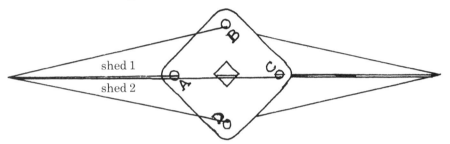

Two tablet positions are used for this:

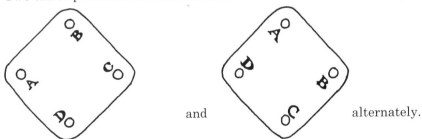

and   alternately.

Take the shuttle from one side through shed 1 and bring it back through shed 2, between each change of shed.

Combining tablet weaving with conventional weaving

A loom is, of course, essential, and it should have two back beams so that the tensions on the two types of weaving can be controlled separately. Alternatively, the tablet weaving warps could be separately weighted.

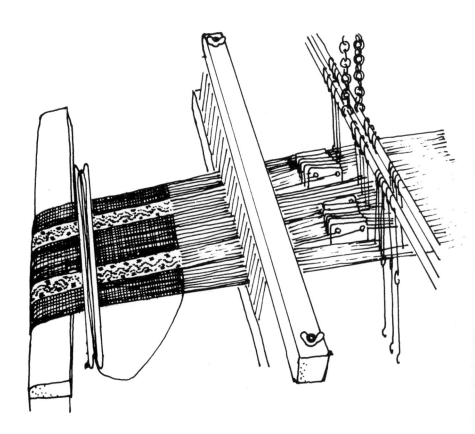

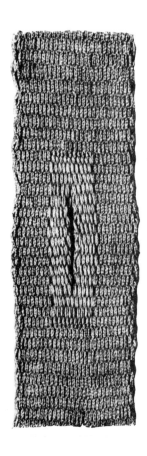

Making a buttonhole

Divide the cards at the point where the buttonhole is to start, and use a separate shuttle for each side. When the slit is long enough, take one shuttle right across and fasten off the other thread. In the photograph a change of colour is shown around the buttonhole, because a slit without some visual definition can look unplanned. This is worked in the same way as (b) in *Variations on one warp*, page 76. It is also possible to weave a pattern around the slit.

Plaited braid

This is produced in the same way as the buttonhole, with several shuttles being used where the braids separate. The three or four bands in the pattern should be hooked on to separate points at the far end, so that when plaiting the braids they can be moved about easily. The braids are then woven as one until the next plaiting point. Although this technique is possible on a loom, it is easier to do with simpler equipment. Wool is not suitable for this type of braid: a non-stretchy cotton thread is ideal.

Two thread weaving

If two threads only are used in a four hole tablet in various combinations (an obvious one is holes 1 and 2, 2 and 3, 3 and 4, 4 and 1) many weaves such as plain, twill and satin can be obtained. A leno (twisted pair of warp threads) weave can also be produced.

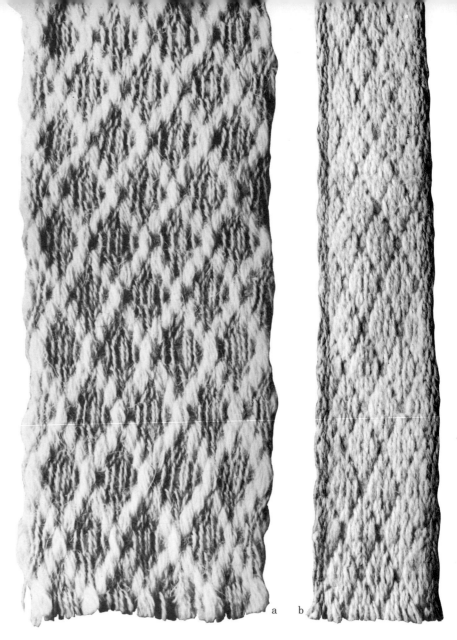

Varying the texture

The texture can be varied by using different thickness (a), or by leaving out some threads altogether (b).

Edging fabric with tablet weaving

The frayed-out warp or weft of a piece of woven fabric becomes the weft of a braid. Experiment with a sample first: the number of ends from the cloth to be taken through the shed each time will depend on the number of threads per 25 mm (1 in.) in the cloth. They can be taken through and back again in the next shed so that the fringe lies back across the fabric.

Some uses for tablet weaving

Bag

This is quickly made with two lengths of 100 mm (4 in.) braid. It needs no fastening device, the longer loop being pushed through the shorter one to form a carrying handle as well as securing the top opening.

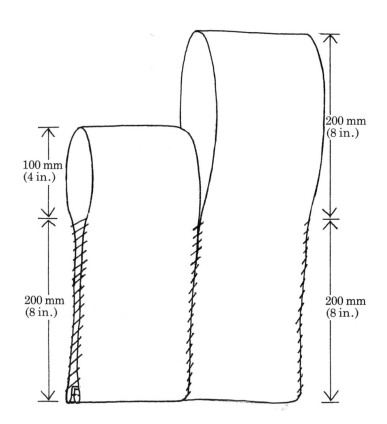

100 mm (4 in.)

200 mm (8 in.)

200 mm (8 in.)

200 mm (8 in.)

Cushions

Several lengths of braid are sewn together to make cushion covers. The seams can be sewn invisibly, or can become an obvious ridge as shown.

Skirt

It is sometimes difficult to get complete integration of fabric and applied bands. By using a knitting machine it is possible to use the same yarns for making the fabric and the braid. The skirt illustrated in the colour plate opposite page 61 was knitted in four panels using the so-called 'weaving' technique. Because it is a shaped skirt, the braid was gently curved into shape as it was sewn on. (See chapter on *How to apply Braids and Fringes*, page 49.)

Bibliography

Byways in Handweaving, Mary Meigs Atwater, Macmillan, New York (one excellent chapter on tablet weaving)

Tablet Weaving, Leaflet 111, Dryad, Leicester

Ciba Review No 117, November 1956, Ciba Limited, Basle, Switzerland (excellent historical survey)

Band, Trotzig and Axelsson, ICA-Förlaget, Västeras, Sweden (one chapter, Swedish text)

Brikvaening, M Hald, Gyldendalske Boghandel, Copenhagen, Denmark (Danish text)

Making Plaits and Braids, June Barker, Batsford London (one chapter)

Le Tissage au Carton dans l'Egypte Ancienne, A Van Gennep and G Jéquiere, Delachaux and Niestle, Neuchatel, Switzerland (French text)

Weaving with Small Appliances: Part Two: Tablet Weaving, Luther Hooper, Pitman, London 1923 (out of print)

Card Weaving, R E Groff, Robin and Russ Handweavers, Oregon

Nauhoja, Merisalo, WSOY Werner Söderstrom Osakeyhtiö, Helsinki, Finland (one chapter, Finnish text)

Uber Brettchenweberei, M Lehmann-Filhés, Dietrich Reimer, Berlin, Germany (German text)

The Bog People, P V Glob, Paladin, London (background to Iron Age tablet weaving)

The Quarterly Journal of Weavers, three articles by Ottfried Staudigel—Nos 38, 40, 52

Suppliers of yarns

UK

Apart from threads such as *Stalite*, *Lyscord*, *Goldfingering*, which are available from wool shops and department stores, some yarns are available by mail only from suppliers of weaving yarns. These yarns are rarely available in quantities of less than $\frac{1}{2}$ lb per colour. Most of these suppliers stock many kinds of yarn in addition to those indicated here as being especially suitable for tablet weaving.

Cotton: 10s/4, 6s/2 Turabast

Craftsman's Mark Ltd
Trefnant
Denbigh LL16 5UD
North Wales

K R Drummond, Bookseller
30 Hart Grove
Ealing Common
London W5
(Callers by appointment only)

Dryads Limited
Northgates
Leicester

2/4s cotton, good colours
'Yarns'
21 Portland Street
Taunton Somerset

Linens and cottons, chenille

William Hall & Co (Monsall) Ltd
177 Stanley Road Cheadle Hulme
Cheadle Cheshire SK8 6RF

Worsted tapestry wools

J Hyslop Bathgate & Co
Victoria Works Galashiels
Scotland

Cotton and wool; stocks vary, sometimes space-dyed

Tesere Yarns
9 Peckover Street Bradford 1

2-fold carpet wool in hanks or thrums (long cut lengths)

The Weavers' Shop
Royal Wilton Carpet Factory
Wilton nr Salisbury Wilts

USA

Contessa Yarns
PO Box 37
Lebanon
Connecticut 06249

Countryside Handweavers
Box 1225
Mission
Kansas 66222

Craft Yarns of Rhode Island Inc
603 Mineral Spring Avenue
Pawtucket Rhode Island 02862

Frederick J Fawcett Inc
129 South Street
Boston Massachusetts

Gary Jones Sheep Farm
RR3 Peabody Kansas

S Achiye Jones
2050 Friendly Eugene
Oregon 97405

Magnolia Weaving
2635-29th Avenue
W, Seattle Washington 98199

Old Mill Yarn
PO Box 115 Eaton Rapids
Michigan 48827

The Silver Shuttle
1301 25th NW Washington DC

The Thread Shed
307 Freeport Road
Pittsburgh Pennsylvania 15215

Suppliers of equipment

The authors have collaborated with Reeves Dryad in the development
of a tablet-weaving kit, made by Reeves and available from leading
department stores and craft material shops throughout the country, or
from Crafts Unlimited (art and craft centres)

178 Kensington High Street
London W8

54 Fleet Street London EC4

13 Charing Cross Road
London EC4

311 Finchley Road London WC2

11/12 Precinct Centre
Oxford Road Manchester 13

11 Knightsbridge Green
London SW1

4 Omnibus Precinct
Newport IOW

202 Bath Street Glasgow C2

21 Macklin Street London WC1

88 Bellgrove Road Welling Kent

also from

Reeves (Canada) Ltd
Downsinew Ontario
Canada

Reeves (Australia) Pty Ltd
Boxhill South Victoria
Australia

Components (tablets, posts and clamps, etc) available from Dryad
Limited, Northgates, Leicester.